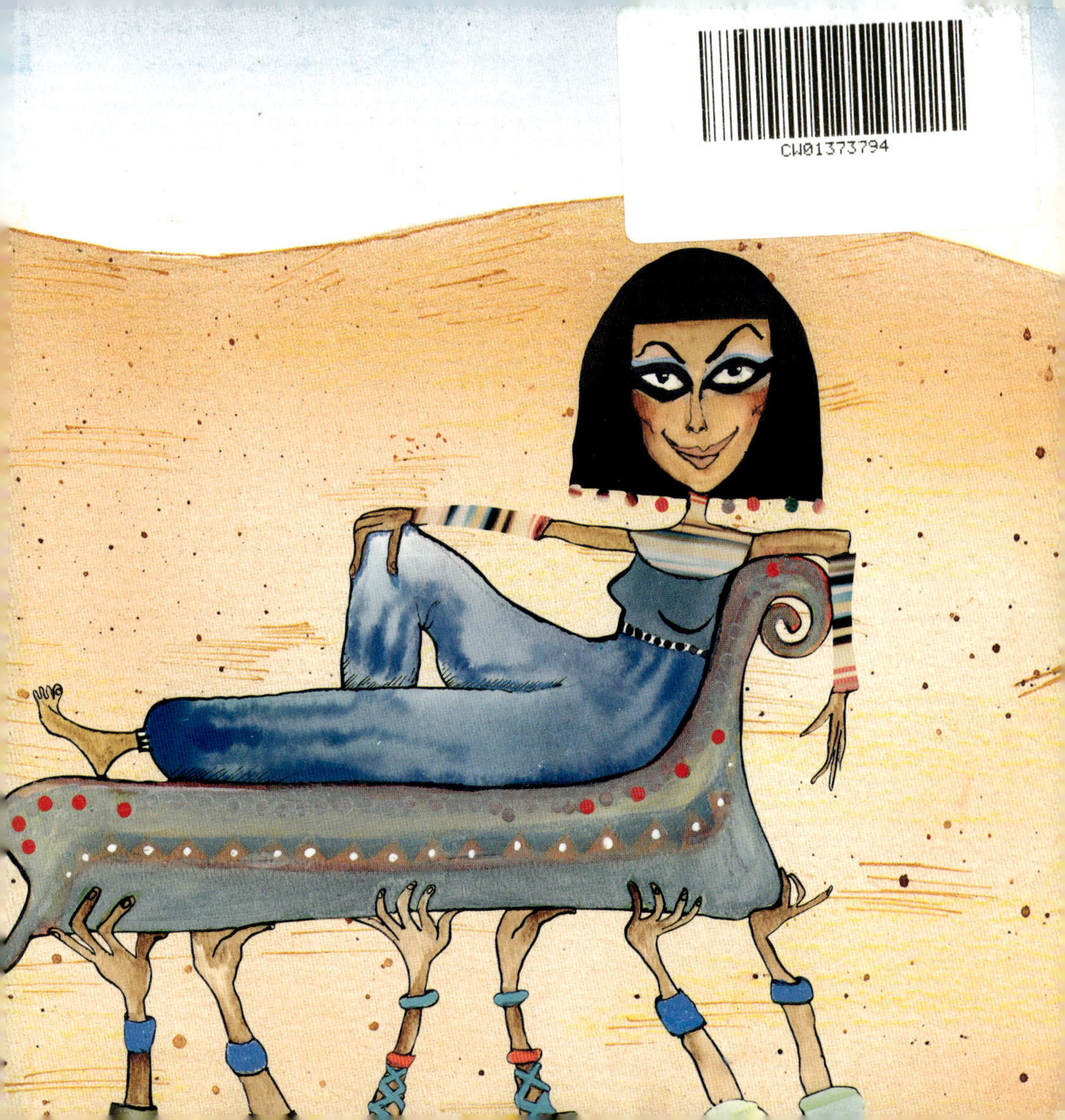

The HOLE Story

Cleopatra

Polly Dunbar

SCHOLASTIC

Cleopatra was beautiful...

intelligent...

and she was the Queen of Egypt.

Julius Caesar ruled the Roman Empire.

When he met Cleopatra...

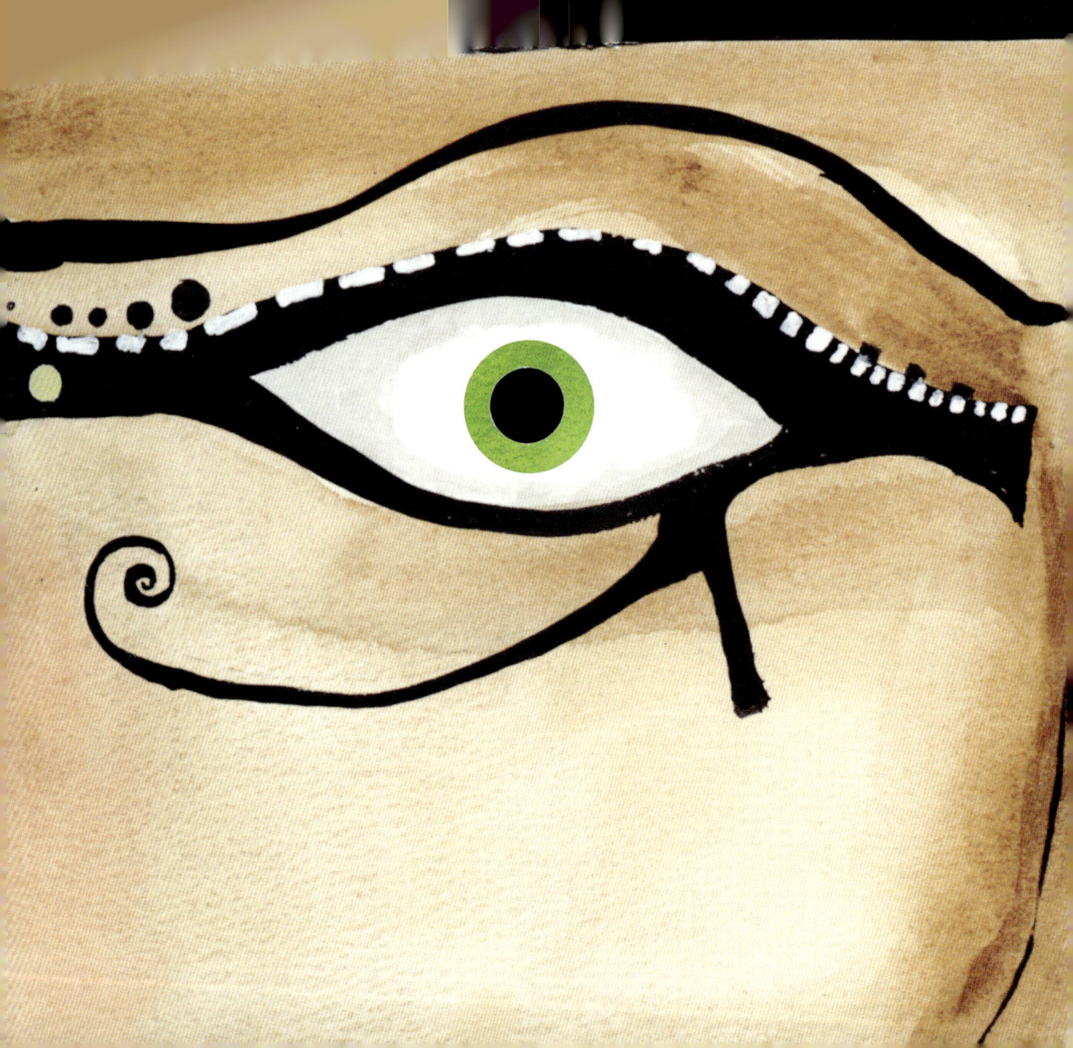

....he was mesmerised.

Julius Caesar and Cleopatra fell in love. Cleopatra thought how great it would be if Egypt and Rome were united too.

ROME

EGYPT

ALEXANDRIA

Especially if their son, Caesarion, could be in charge.

But Julius Caesar was killed by his enemies in Rome.

Cleopatra ran back to Egypt with baby Caesarion.

Mark Anthony and Octavian became the new rulers of the Roman Empire. Cleopatra returned to Rome to meet them.

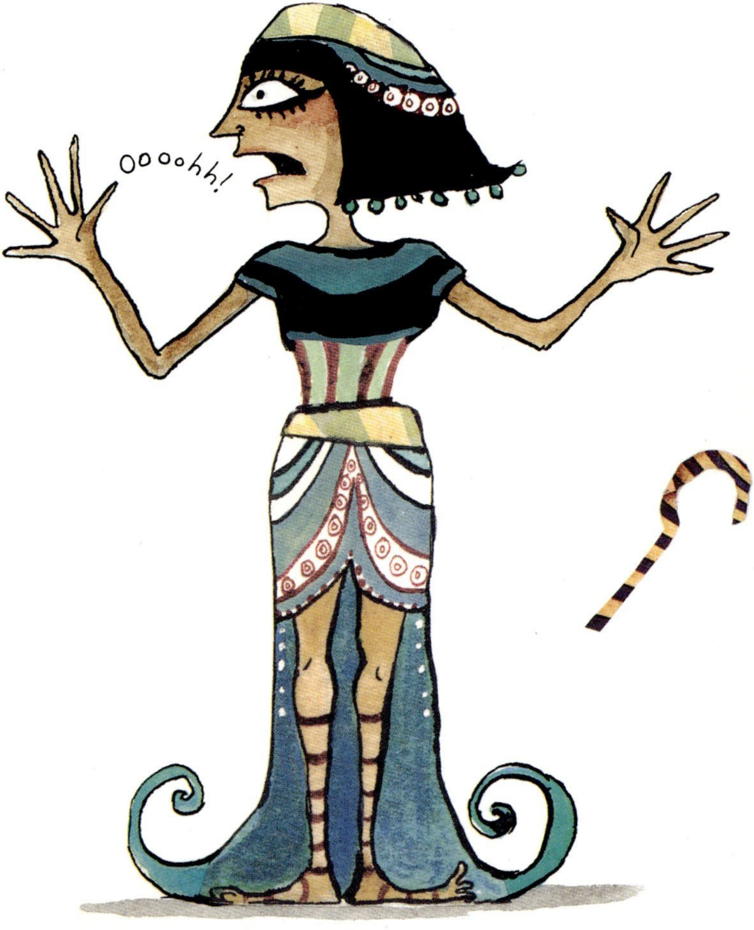
Ooooohh!

Octavian now ruled Rome on his own.
He asked Cleopatra over.

But by now Cleopatra, the last Queen of Egypt, really had died...

EGYPT

NILE

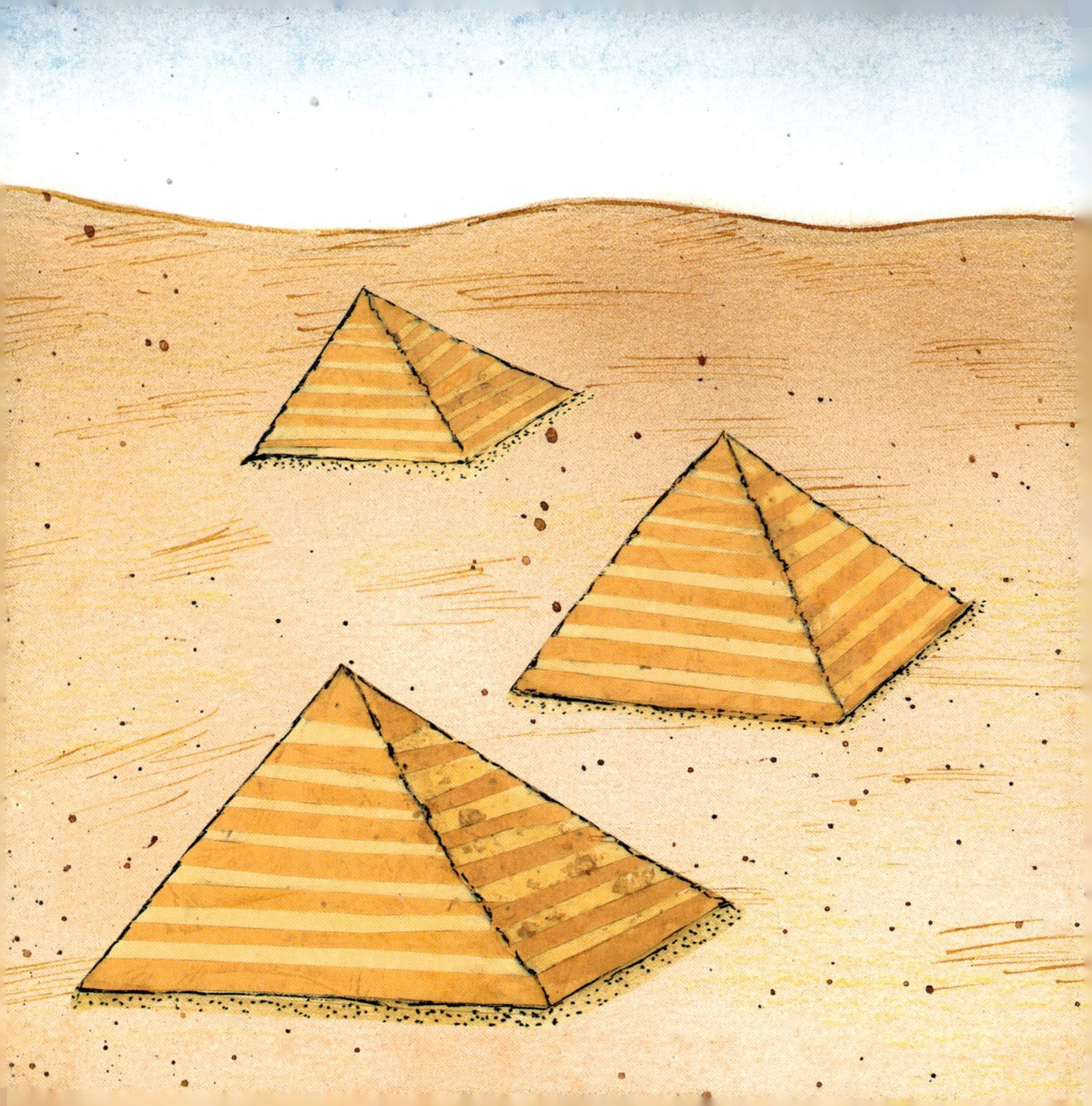

...no one is quite sure how.